FACT?

FACT OR FICTION?

FICTION?

Buffalo Bill Cody

Marcia Amidon
Lusted

Mitchell Lane
PUBLISHERS
P.O. Box 196
Hockessin, DE 19707
www.mitchelllane.com

Mitchell Lane
PUBLISHERS

Printing   1   2   3   4   5   6   7   8

Audie Murphy   Francis Marion
Buffalo Bill Cody   Robin Hood
The Buffalo Soldiers   The Tuskegee Airmen
Eliot Ness   Wyatt Earp

Library of Congress Cataloging-in-Publication Data
Lusted, Marcia Amidon.
 Buffalo Bill Cody / by Marcia Amidon Lusted.
    pages cm. — (Fact or fiction?)
 Includes bibliographical references and index.
 Audience: Grades 3–6.
 ISBN 978-1-61228-960-1 (library bound)
1. Buffalo Bill, 1846–1917—Juvenile literature. 2. Pioneers—West (U.S.)—Biography—Juvenile literature. 3. Entertainers—United States—Biography—Juvenile literature. 4. Buffalo Bill's Wild West Show—History—Juvenile literature. 5. West (U.S.)—Biography—Juvenile literature. I. Title.
 F594.L96 2016
 978'.02092—dc23
 [B]

                                                  2015010441

eBook ISBN: 978-1-61228-961-8

PBP

CONTENTS

Chapter 1
The Wild West......................................5

Chapter 2
A Boy from Iowa..............................9

Chapter 3
Becoming Buffalo Bill....................13

Chapter 4
The Wild West Show......................17

Chapter 5
The End of the Road.......................23

Fact or Fiction?....................................26
Chapter Notes.....................................28
Glossary...30
Works Consulted.................................31
Further Reading..................................31
On the Internet...................................31
Index..32

Words in **bold** throughout can be found in the Glossary.

Buffalo Bill, around 1892, with his famous buckskin jacket, saddle, and rifle.

The Wild West

The Wild West frontier in the United States was disappearing by the 1880s. The once-open **ranges** were filling up with farms. Many Native Americans had been forced to leave their traditional lands and move onto reservations. Cattle no longer roamed freely across the open **prairie**. The huge herds of buffalo had shrunken. But Americans still thought of the Wild West as a romantic, adventurous place.[1] One of the main reasons why people's imaginations were still captivated by cowboys and Indian attacks and buffalo hunts was a man named William F. Cody, who had become famous under the nickname of Buffalo Bill.

Cody led an adventurous life and acquired a national reputation as a writer and actor. So he decided to use his experiences, his **showmanship** skills, and the stories he had created about the West to create a new kind of entertainment called Buffalo Bill's Wild West Show. It opened in 1883 and had traditional elements from traveling circuses, such as horseback riding tricks and **exotic** animals, and added many things American audiences had never seen before: **sharpshooters**, **reenactments** of famous Native American attacks, a simulated Pony Express ride, a buffalo hunt, and more.

For Americans who lived in cities and worked in offices or factories, Buffalo Bill's show gave them a taste of the adventures they couldn't have in real life and became one of the most popular entertainments of its time. As the real Western frontier became just a memory, people happily paid to see Buffalo Bill's version.[2] In 1886, more than one million people in New York City alone saw it. Soon the show was entertaining audiences who weren't even American. It played in European cities like London, Rome, Barcelona, and Paris. Its popularity helped create the legends and myths of the Wild West for people all over the world.

The Wild West Show lasted for 30 years and made Buffalo Bill one of the most famous Americans in the world. He also became a businessman. He invested the money he earned from his show in things like oil, coal, and even making movies and publishing. He founded the town of Cody, Wyoming in 1895 and built a hotel there.

He also became an advocate for Native Americans. Even though his show featured reenactments of famous Native American battles, he once said, "Every Indian outbreak that I have ever known has resulted from broken promises and broken treaties by the government."[3] He worked to get better treatment for them. He also spoke out about conserving buffalo, even though he had killed thousands of them when he was younger.

Most people who saw his show thought that they were seeing real American history. Buffalo Bill saw that people wanted stories of the Wild West and heroes to go with them. But he created a legendary picture of what the Wild West was like. This picture wasn't always true. Even Buffalo Bill himself wasn't exactly how he **portrayed** himself. He created a version of his life that was even more exciting and adventurous. Because he was so good at storytelling and creating his version of his life and the Wild West, it can be very difficult to tell what is true and what is exaggerated. Even today, historians argue about whether some of Buffalo Bill's most famous **exploits** actually took place. Just what is fact, and what is fiction?

Buffalo Bill fires his rifle into the air during a 1907 show. His Wild West Show included many Native American cast members.

William F. Cody used his experiences as a Pony Express rider and Army scout to create his identity as Buffalo Bill.

CHAPTER 2

A Boy from Iowa

William F. Cody was born in 1846 in Scott County, Iowa. He grew up on the prairie, learning to ride and shoot. He did not spend a lot of time in school. When his father died in 1857, William was the oldest boy in his family. He took on the responsibility of providing for his mother and his brothers and sisters.[1] He went to work as a messenger boy for a freight company. Later he took a job herding oxen and cattle. He rode with a wagon train as a driver and a **wrangler**, herding cattle and horses. He even tried his luck during the gold rush near Pike's Peak in 1859, although he didn't have much success.

In 1860, Cody got a job that would eventually become one of the biggest pieces of his story. He may have seen an ad placed in western newspapers: "Wanted. Young, skinny wiry fellows not over 18. Must be expert riders, willing to risk death daily. Orphans preferred. Wages 25.00 per week."[2]

The ad was **recruiting** riders for the Pony Express. This was a new way to deliver mail and information quickly between St. Joseph, Missouri and Sacramento, California. Riders would push their mounts to a full gallop and change horses at stations placed about ten miles (sixteen kilometers) apart, traveling 75–100 miles a day. Cody was 14 and already good at riding, shooting, and dealing with conditions on the frontier. He rode for the Pony Express until it went out of business in October, 1861.

Cody's mother died in 1863. Soon afterward, he began working as a scout for the Union Army during the Civil War. He took part in battles against the Kiowa and Comanche tribes of Native Americans. He eventually enlisted in the 7th Kansas **Cavalry** and became an actual soldier, although he still worked as a scout. In his autobiography, he tells the story of two adventures during his time in the Army. One was an unexpected meeting with the famous lawman Wild Bill Hickok, and the other was protecting a mother and her three daughters who were afraid that they would be attacked and robbed by Union soldiers. Like some of his other stories, no one is sure if these two really took place.

Cody got married in 1866, to Louisa Frederici. They would eventually have four children. But for now he kept working for the US Army as a scout and message carrier. Cody left the Army the following year and began hunting buffalo to feed the construction crews building the Kansas Pacific railroad. It was during this time that he got the nickname "Buffalo Bill," because he said he killed more than 4,000 buffalo in seventeen months. Another man, William Comstock, also claimed that nickname. According to Cody, he and Comstock had an eight-hour-long shooting match. Cody won, and earned the sole right to the title of Buffalo Bill.

This 1875 portrait shows Buffalo Bill in the costume he wore for the stage play about his life.

He returned to Army life in 1868, working as chief of scouts. He took part in numerous battles against native tribes over the course of several years, a period sometimes called the Indian Wars. Buffalo Bill was an expert **tracker** and fighter, and in 1872 he was awarded the Medal of Honor. This is the nation's highest military honor. His commanding officer said, "Mr. William Cody's reputation for bravery and skill as a guide is so well established that I need not say anything else but that he acted in his usual manner."[3] He was one of only four civilian scouts ever to receive this honor.

Buffalo Bill Cody had earned a reputation for being brave and skillful. He had also been through many amazing experiences and adventures. But the same things were true of many men in the exciting days of the Wild West. How did he make himself different from those other men and become Buffalo Bill, legend and showman?

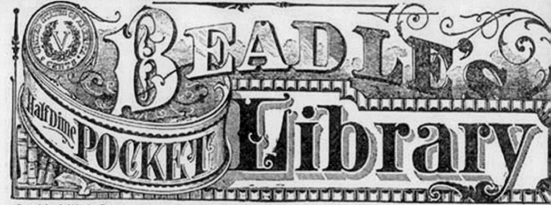

Copyrighted, 1881, by Beadle and Adams. Entered at the Post Office at New York, N. Y., as Second Class Mail Matter. Feb. 20, 188

Vol. I. &2.50 a Year.   Published Weekly by Beadle and Adams, No. 98 William St., New York.   Price, Five Cents.   No.

THE PRAIRIE PILOT; or, THE PHANTOM SPY

BY BUFFALO BILL.

This cover, from one of the hundreds of dime novels written about Buffalo Bill, promises an exciting story. Few of them were actually written by him.

EXAMINING THE CREVICES IN THE WALL OF ROCK, PRAIRIE PILOT FOUND ONE THAT LOOKED INTO

CHAPTER 3

Becoming Buffalo Bill

Williiam Cody began his transformation into the popular Buffalo Bill legend when he met Ned Buntline in 1869. Buntline was a writer who had started a magazine called *Ned Buntline's Own* in the 1840s. It was filled with outrageous, adventurous, thrilling stories that weren't always truthful. Those stories were popular, and soon he began writing dime novels. Dime novels were short books that usually focused on the dramatic, daring adventures of a single character. They had bright covers and usually sold for only a nickel or a dime. Buntline became known as "The King of the Dime Novels" and made a lot of money from writing them.

After meeting Cody, who was still working as a scout and hunting buffalo, Buntline decided to write a book about him, called *Buffalo Bill, the King of the Frontier Men*.[1] Of course, it exaggerated Buffalo Bill's western experiences, but the public loved it. Up to this point the Buffalo Bill nickname had been largely regional. Now it became national, and was so popular that Buntline turned it into a stage play in 1872 called *The Scouts of the Prairie*. He convinced Cody to travel to Chicago and play himself in the show. Cody wasn't a very good actor, but his mere presence on stage brought in bigger audiences.[2] He began to realize that people loved tales of the Wild West, and that his real-life adventures combined with the ones Buntline made up created the character of Buffalo Bill. The two men eventually stopped working together, but not until Buffalo Bill spent eleven seasons of acting in between trips west for hunting expeditions. He also began his own career as an author, writing his autobiography and some of his own Buffalo Bill dime novels. Eventually there were 1,700 of these dime novels, though most of them were written by other authors and just had Buffalo Bill's name on them.

Buffalo Bill's cabinet card, taken in 1894. These were often given out for publicity or as business cards.

These dime novels made Buffalo Bill's life sound exciting, and yet at the same time, very American. People who read these books believed they told the truth, even though they were most often only partly accurate. But the excitement, adventure, and true American West feeling made them popular. As Col. Prentiss Ingraham, who wrote many Buffalo Bill books, pointed out:

"The land of America is full of romance, and tales that stir the blood can be told over and over again of bold Privateers and reckless Buccaneers who have swept along the coasts; of fierce naval battles, sea chases, daring smugglers; and on shore of brave deeds in the saddle and afoot; of red trails followed to the bitter end and savage encounters in forest wilds. Who has not heard the name of Buffalo Bill—a magic name, seemingly, to every boy's heart? Buffalo Bill will go down to history as one of America's strange heroes who has loved the trackless wilds, rolling plains and mountain solitudes of our land, far more than the bustle and turmoil, the busy life and joys of our cities, and who has stood as a barrier between civilization and savagery, risking his own life to save the lives of others.[3]"

These dime novels not only created the legend of Buffalo Bill, but also made him a **celebrity**. He was already a popular entertainer on stage, and the books about his exploits reached even more people. Without them, he almost certainly would not have become as famous as he did.

Buffalo Bill continued working as a scout through 1876, and would serve again in 1890 when there was another series of Native American **uprisings**. He used some of his experiences as a scout to add to the stage plays he was in. He was good at taking the bare bones of an event and making it far more dramatic and **sensational**. Because of the success of these stage adventures, Buffalo Bill decided it was time to organize his own show.

15

BUFFALO BILL'S

WILD WEST

COL. W. F. CODY

PROGRAMME 1D.

The program cover for Buffalo Bill's Wild West show, 1894.

The Wild West Show

For decades, traveling circuses, with exotic animals and horseback riders doing tricks, had been popular entertainments in the United States. It also seems likely that Buffalo Bill had seen at least one. In 1872, legendary frontiersman Wild Bill Hickok staged a show with cowboys and Native Americans and buffalo in Niagara Falls. Buffalo Bill built on these shows and his own reputation to create an outdoor extravaganza that broke new ground in the field of entertainment.

The first show, "Cody and Carver's Golden West," made its debut on May 19, 1883, in Omaha, Nebraska. During his first season, Buffalo Bill partnered with Dr. W.F. Carver, a dentist and successful sharpshooter who had performed in other **exhibitions**. For these first shows, Buffalo Bill arranged for a tribe of Pawnee to perform, found an old stagecoach, and collected mules, horses, and other animals. The show included acts like **marksmanship** by Buffalo Bill and Carver, a bareback pony race, an exhibition of the kind of riding done by the Pony Express riders, steer roping, and recreations of events like a hunt on the plains and an attack on a stagecoach.

Buffalo Bill and Dr. Carver did not get along well, and split up after one season.[1] Buffalo Bill continued with what was now called "Buffalo Bill's Wild West Show." While his success prompted other people to begin creating similar shows, his always remained the most popular. The public already knew who he was from his stage performances and dime novels. In just a few years, his show was making a hundred thousand dollars a year from ticket sales.[2] There were buffalo

hunts, and recreations of Indian attacks on a stagecoach that included real Native Americans. He featured attractions like Annie Oakley, a champion sharpshooter who could hit targets when shooting backwards with only a mirror reflection to help her aim. For one season, the show even included the legendary Native American chief Sitting Bull. One of the featured events in the show was a

A publicity photo of champion sharpshooter Annie Oakley around 1899. She was one of the star attractions of Buffalo Bill's Wild West show.

recreation of Custer's Last Stand, or the Battle of Little Bighorn in 1876. The show included real Lakota Native Americans who had supposedly fought in the actual battle. Of course, the staged version of these events was part history and part entertainment, similar to the way that Hollywood movies often gloss over or change actual events to make them more entertaining.[3]

Audiences and even critics thought they were seeing actual frontier history. One critic wrote, "It is not a show. It is a resurrection . . . of the honest features of wild Western life and pioneer incidents . . . that men, women, and children may see, realize, understand, and forever remember what the Western pioneers met, encountered, and overcame."[4]

Buffalo Bill became an international celebrity in 1892, when the Wild West Show toured Europe. Buffalo Bill's partner, Nate Salsbury, added "and the Congress of Rough Riders of the World" to the title so that the show could include **Cossacks**, **lancers**, and other military troupes from different countries.

This poster for the Wild West show features some of the Rough Riders and foreign soldiers who had joined the show.

The huge cast of the Wild West show sets sail from New York City to London in 1887.

Buffalo Bill decided to set up his show in Chicago, Illinois, during the World's Columbian Exposition the following year. The Exposition was a world's fair that featured exhibitions and attractions from both the United States and all over the world. Buffalo Bill was supposedly refused permission to be part of the exposition's **midway**. But he made more money during the six months of the exhibition by setting up outside where the other midway rides were not competing with him.

Buffalo Bill's show kept growing, adding more attractions like sideshows, Arabian **acrobats**, dancing elephants, and high divers. These ideas for acts were borrowed from circuses as an attempt to keep audiences interested in the shows. By the mid-1890s, it took two trains with fifty railroad cars each to transport the show's five hundred cast and crew members, equipment, supplies, and animals. The performers, including twenty-five cowboys, twelve cowgirls, and one hundred Native American men, women, and children, slept in tents or on the railroad cars. In 1899, the show traveled 11,000 miles in 200 days and gave 341 performances in 132 cities across America.

But he soon faced a new and intriguing form of entertainment: the movies. Would Buffalo Bill, the famous showman, survive the change?

Buffalo Bill, shown around 1907, as the popularity of his Wild West show declined and he began making movies.

CHAPTER 5

The End of the Road

As the twentieth century dawned, movies were becoming increasingly popular. And the Wild West suddenly seemed more real on a screen than it did in a live exhibition like Buffalo Bill's Wild West Show. For a while Buffalo Bill seemed to be making the transition to the movies. In 1898 and 1912, he actually starred in two silent movies about himself.[1] But the public began losing interest in some of the old western legends. Cowboys and Native Americans would always be popular subjects for movies, but the old Wild West shows were dying away. If audiences wanted to see roping and riding skills, they went to rodeos, which were much less expensive to produce than big traveling shows.

Buffalo Bill's Wild West Show began to suffer financially. In 1908, he sold part of the show to Gordon William Lillie—popularly known as Pawnee Bill—who had a competing "Wild West and Great Far East Show." The two men traveled together as partners, but after five seasons their combined show went **bankrupt**.[2] While Cody had made a fortune from his show business career, he later lost it because he invested his money poorly and did not manage it well.

After the end of his show, William Cody tried one last project based on his western experiences. He produced a movie called *The Indian Wars*. It reenacted the battles from the Indian Wars which he had participated in, filmed on their original sites. Cody wanted the film to be historically correct and to have roles played by actual participants and not actors. This was a challenge for everyone involved. It meant that Buffalo Bill had to recreate things he did when he was thirty, even though he was now sixty-seven. The filming took almost two months. It was released to the public in many different versions. Some included **footage** from the Buffalo Bill Wild West shows, and others were strictly about the Indian Wars alone. Unfortunately, the movie was never very popular and the original film footage has been lost.

William "Buffalo Bill" Cody died on January 10, 1917, while he was visiting his sister in Denver, Colorado. He was buried on Lookout Mountain, west of Denver, which overlooks the Great Plains. Annie Oakley wrote of him, "Goodbye, old friend. The sun setting over the mountains will pay its tribute to the resting place of the last of the great builders of the West, all of which you loved, and part of which you were."[3] Even though he ended his life bankrupt, he had created a mythical version of himself that would never die. He not only shared his version of the Wild West and the frontier days from his own experiences, but also made himself part of that version of history. He is a mixture of fact and fiction that is almost impossible to separate because he combined the two

Buffalo Bill's monument on Lookout Mountain, west of Denver, Colorado. His wife Louisa is buried with him.

so well. Many of the things that regularly appear in Western movies come from the version of the West that Buffalo Bill created. His image as a rugged frontiersman wearing buckskin leggings, a fringed coat, and a broad-brimmed hat while carrying a rifle, has become part of American history.

FACT OR FICTION?

Buffalo Bill's life is a combination of what he really experienced, and the way in which he took some of those experiences and changed or embellished them to create better stories. He was very good at entertaining and he knew what his audiences wanted: exciting, adventurous stories of the Wild West, but not necessarily the way they actually happened. He used his experiences as an Army scout, a Pony Express rider, and a buffalo hunter as a basis for creating the kinds of entertainment that people loved.

He is important because he helped create the image of the Wild West that we still have today. Many of the things he included in his stories, stage plays, and Wild West Show would become basic ingredients of all Western stories and movies: stagecoach attacks, Pony Express riders, cowboys, Indian wars, and buffalo wandering the Great Plains. And despite his tales of Native American battles and buffalo hunts, he later became an advocate for native peoples and tried to preserve the fast-disappearing buffalo herds.

William "Buffalo Bill" Cody's life is a combination of fact and fiction. Sometimes it's hard to tell the difference between what actually happened and the version of events that he wrote about and added to his shows. It is even more difficult because there were more than a thousand dime novels written about Buffalo Bill, and most of those stories were completely made up. But he helped create one of America's most important cultural identities, the Wild West. Until the invention of movies, which replaced many live shows, it was one of the only opportunities for people to get a taste of the Wild West life.

His shows also brought the American West to people all over the world as he toured Europe and introduced new audiences to all the elements of the Wild West image. He helped Americans remember the West at a time when it was fast disappearing. He also fed their longing for stories of the frontier and exploration, when many Americans were moving from the country to the cities, and from farming to factory jobs. And that is why he is still remembered today. Buffalo Bill gave us the image of the West and a young America that we still treasure as part of our history.

Chapter 1: The Wild West

1. Chuck Wills, *Annie Oakley: A Photographic Story of a Life* (New York: DK Publishing), 2007, pp. 52–53.
2. Ibid., p. 56.
3. *Old West Legends: Buffalo Bill Cody - Trapper, Trader & Frontiersman*. Legends of America, 2003. http://www.legendsofamerica.com/we-buffalobill.html

Chapter 2: A Boy from Iowa

1. Robert A. Carter, *Buffalo Bill Cody: The Man Behind the Legend* (New York: John Wiley & Sons, Inc., 2000), pp. 24–25.
2. Sharon Shahid, "150 Years Ago in News History: The Pony Express Takes a Ride." *Newseum*, April 1, 2010. http://www.newseum.org/news/2010/04/150-years-ago-in-news-history-the-pony-express-takes-a-ride.html
3. William F. "Buffalo Bill" Cody. Iowa Medal of Honor Winners. http://iowahistory.org/museum/exhibits/medal-of-honor/sf-03-cody-iw/index.htm

Chapter 3: Becoming Buffalo Bill

1. "March 20, 1823: Ned Buntline born." This Day in History: Old West. http://www.history.com/this-day-in-history/ned-buntline-born
2. Chuck Wills, *Annie Oakley: A Photographic Story of a Life* (New York: DK Publishing), 2007, pp. 52–53.
3. Col. Prentiss Ingraham, *Adventures of Buffalo Bill from Boyhood to Manhood*. New York: Beadle and Adams, 1882. http://www-sul.stanford.edu/depts/dp/pennies/texts/ingraham1_toc.html

Chapter 4: The Wild West Show

1. Joy S. Kasson, *Buffalo Bill's Wild West: Celebrity, Memory, and Popular History* (New York: Farrar, Strauss and Giroux, 2000), p. 44.
2. "Buffalo Bill." *The American Experience*, PBS. http://www.pbs.org/wgbh/americanexperience/features/transcript/cody-transcript/
3. Dickinson, Greg, Brian L. Ott, and Eric Aoki. "Memory and Myth at the Buffalo Bill Museum." *Western Journal of Communication*, April 2005. http://www.tandfonline.com/doi/abs/10.1080/10570310500076684?journalCode=rwjc20#preview
4. Kasson, *Buffalo Bill's Wild West*, p. 61.

Chapter 5: The End of the Road

1. Chris Smallbone, "Buffalo Bill." nativeamerican.co.uk, March 2006. http://www.nativeamerican.co.uk/bbill.html
2. "Old West Legends: Buffalo Bill Cody—Trapper, Trader & Frontiersman." Legends of America, 2003. http://www.legendsofamerica.com/we-buffalobill.html
3. Chuck Wills, *Annie Oakley: A Photographic Story of a Life* (New York: DK Publishing, 2007), p. 95.

acrobats (AK-roe-bats)—people skilled at actions or stunts such as swinging from a trapeze or tightrope walking

bankrupt (BANGK-rupt)—completely without money, legally declared unable to pay debts

cavalry (KAV-uhl-ree)—soldiers trained to fight on horseback

celebrity (suh-LEHB-ruh-tee)—a famous person

Cossacks (CAHSS-aks)—people living in southern Russia, especially noted for skilled horsemanship and military prowess

exhibition (ek-suh-BISH-un)—a display for the public

exotic (eg-ZAH-tik)—foreign, strange, unusual

exploit (ECK-sploit)—a verya brave or daring act

footage (FUHT-idg)—a length of film made for movies or television

invest (in-VEST)—put money to use to earn interest or make a profit

lancers (LAN-suhrs)—cavalrymen equipped with long spears called lances

marksmanship (MARKS-muhn-ship)—skill in shooting at a target

midway (MIHD-way)—area of a fair, carnival or circus where rides and amusements are located

portrayed (por-TRAYD)—played the part of

prairie (PRAYER-ee)—a wide area of flat or rolling ground with tall grass and few trees

ranges (RAYN-juhz)—expanses of open land where livestock can wander and graze

recruiting (ree-KROOT-ing)—persuading a person to join something

reenactments (ree-uhn-ACT-ments)—performing new versions of old events, usually in a theatrical performance

sensational (sen-SAY-shuh-nuhl)—causing excitement

sharpshooter (SHARP-shoo-tuhr)—person who is very skilled at shooting

showmanship (SHO-man-ship)—the ability to do something or present things theatrically or dramatically

tracker (TRA-kuhr)—someone who follows footprints or other signs of trails

uprisings (UP-rie-zings)—revolts against a government or its policies

wrangler (RANG-luhr)—a person in charge of horses or other livestock

Carter, Robert A. *Buffalo Bill Cody: The Man Behind the Legend*. New York: John Wiley and Sons, 2000.

Cody, William F. *Buffalo Bill's Life Story: An Autobiography*. Reprint edition. New York: Skyhorse Press, 2010.

Corbett, Christopher. *Orphans Preferred: The Twisted Truth and Lasting Legend of the Pony Express*. New York: Broadway Books, 2003.

Kasson, Joy S. *Buffalo Bill's Wild West: Celebrity, Memory, and Popular History*. New York: Farrar, Strauss and Giroux, 2000.

Wills, Chuck. *Annie Oakley: A Photographic Story of a Life*. New York: DK Publishing, 2007.

FURTHER READING

Coerr, Eleanor. *Buffalo Bill and the Pony Express*. New York: HarperCollins, 1996.

D'aulaire, Ingri Parim. *Buffalo Bill*. San Luis Obispo, CA: Beautiful Feet Books, 1998.

Harness, Cheryl. *They're Off!: The Story of the Pony Express*. New York: Simon & Schuster, 2002.

Reis, Ronald A. *Legends of the Wild West: Buffalo Bill Cody*. New York: Chelsea House, 2010.

Sanford, William R. *Buffalo Bill Cody: Courageous Wild West Showman*. Berkeley Heights, NJ: Enslow Publishers, 2012.

Spinner, Stephanie. *Who Was Annie Oakley?* New York: Penguin, 2002.

Stevenson, Augusta. *Buffalo Bill: Frontier Daredevil*. New York: Simon & Schuster, 1991.

ON THE INTERNET

"Introduction: Buffalo Bill." The American Experience, PBS. http://www.pbs.org/wgbh/americanexperience/films/cody/

"Old West Legends: Buffalo Bill Cody—Trapper, Trader & Frontiersman." Legends of America, 2003. http://www.legendsofamerica.com/we-buffalobill.html

Fees, Paul. "Wild West shows: Buffalo Bill's Wild West." Buffalo Bill Center of the West. http://centerofthewest.org/learn/western-essays/wild-west-shows/

7th Kansas Cavalry 10
Battle of Little Bighorn 19
Buffalo Bill 4, 5, 10, 11, 13, 15, 19, 20, 22
Buffalo Bill, the King of the Frontier Men 13
Buffalo Bill's Wild West Show 6, 16, 18, 19, 23, 24
buffalo hunting 6, 10, 13, 18
Buntline, Ned 13
Carver, Dr. W.F. 17, 18
Cody and Carver's Golden West 17
Cody, William F. 5, 7, 9, 11, 13, 23, 24, 26
Comanche 10
Comstock, William 10
Congress of Rough Riders 19
Custer's Last Stand 19
dime novels 12, 14, 15
Frederici, Louise 10
gold rush 9
Hickok, Wild Bill 10, 17

Indian Wars movie 24
Indian Wars 11, 15
Ingraham, Prentiss 15
Iowa 9
Kansas Pacific Railroad 10
Kiowa 10
Lakota 19
Lillie, Gordon William 23
Medal of Honor 11
movies 19, 21, 23, 24
Native Americans 6, 7, 15, 21, 23, 26
Oakley, Annie 18, 24
Pawnee Bill 23
Pawnee 17
Pony Express 6, 8, 9, 10, 17
Salsbury, Nate 19
sharpshooters 5, 18
Sitting Bull 18
The Scouts of the Prairie 13
US Army 10, 11, 15
Wild West 5, 7, 11, 14, 26
World's Columbian Exposition 20

ABOUT THE AUTHOR

Marcia Amidon Lusted has written over 100 books for young readers, and 450 magazine articles. She is an editor for Cricket Media. She lives in New Hampshire. Her great-grandfather once met Buffalo Bill and went to his Wild West Show. Visit her at www.adventuresinnonfiction.com for more information about her books.